W9-AOB-075

How the West was Won

Written by Nicola Barber
Illustrated by David McAllister

p

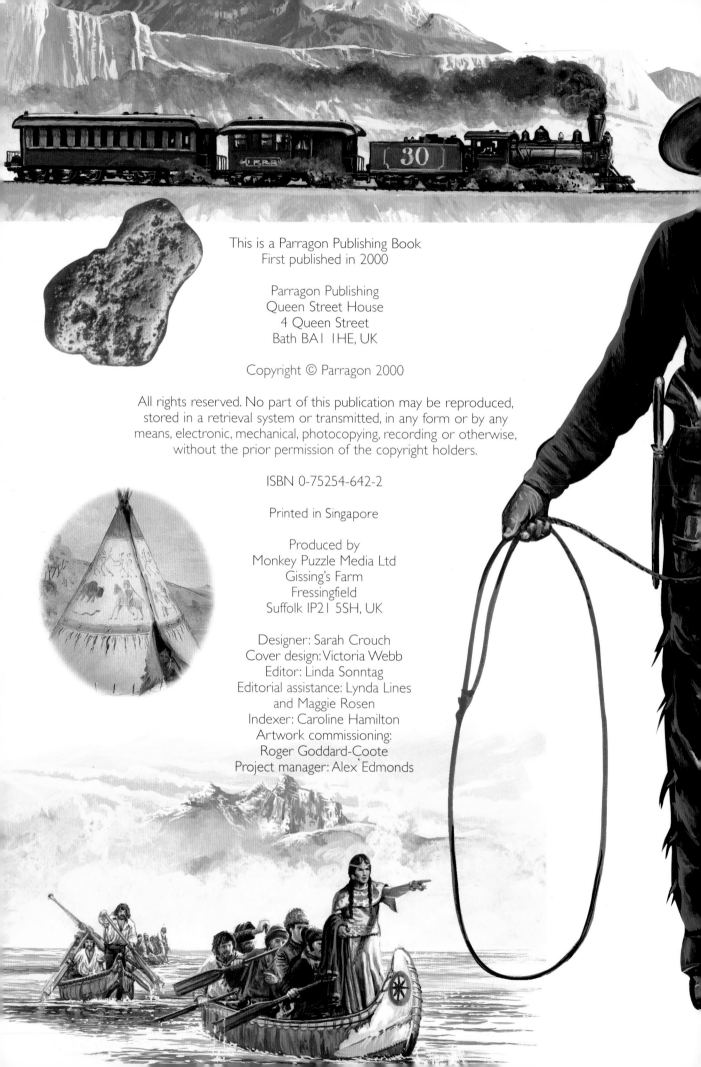

This is a Parragon Publishing Book
First published in 2000

Parragon Publishing
Queen Street House
4 Queen Street
Bath BA1 1HE, UK

Copyright © Parragon 2000

All rights reserved. No part of this publication may be reproduced,
stored in a retrieval system or transmitted, in any form or by any
means, electronic, mechanical, photocopying, recording or otherwise,
without the prior permission of the copyright holders.

ISBN 0-75254-642-2

Printed in Singapore

Produced by
Monkey Puzzle Media Ltd
Gissing's Farm
Fressingfield
Suffolk IP21 5SH, UK

Designer: Sarah Crouch
Cover design: Victoria Webb
Editor: Linda Sonntag
Editorial assistance: Lynda Lines
and Maggie Rosen
Indexer: Caroline Hamilton
Artwork commissioning:
Roger Goddard-Coote
Project manager: Alex Edmonds

Contents

Who lived in the West?

WHEN EUROPEANS FIRST ARRIVED IN THE "NEW WORLD" OF THE Americas, they did not move to an empty continent. This land had been home to millions of Native Americans for a thousand generations or more. There were over 200 different tribes in the West, speaking over 75 different languages. They included the Hopi, Clatsop, Pawnee, Mojave, Nez Perce, Shoshone, Chinook, and Zuni. Each of these peoples had their own traditions, customs and ways of life.

Who lived on the Plateau?
Bordered by the Cascade Range to the west and the Rocky Mountains to the east, the Plateau region was home to tribes such as the Chinook, the Northern Shoshone, Nez Perce, and the Kootenai. The peoples of the Plateau caught salmon in the Columbia and Fraser rivers as well as foraging for camas roots and other vegetables.

Who built houses of bark and reeds?
On the Pacific coast, the Native Americans in California built small shelters from reeds, others made tepee-like structures from the bark of the redwood tree. Further north, tribes such as the Nootka and the Haida made sturdy rectangular houses from planks of wood, tied together with cords.

What was a potlatch?

A potlatch was a ceremony held by the tribes of the Pacific Northwest such as the Tlingit and Chinook. It was a spectacular occasion when gifts were given away, people dressed in their finest clothes, and there was much feasting and celebration.

What were shells used for?

The tribes along the Pacific coast used the beautiful shells of oysters, clams and other shellfish as a kind of money. They exchanged shells for goods. Some shells ended up thousands of miles away from the coast, worn as ornaments by people who had never been anywhere near the sea.

Who lived in multi-level housing?

The peoples of the hot, dry southwest lived in settlements called pueblos. They built large living complexes out of adobe (mud brick) in which they lived all year round. The tribes of this area included the Zuni, the Acoma, and the Hopi.

This tepee was home to a family of Crow tribespeople. The decorations on the outside show events from hunting and battles.

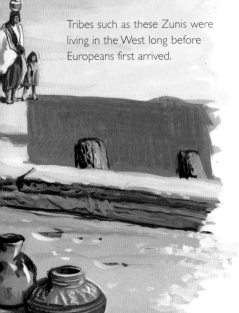

Tribes such as these Zunis were living in the West long before Europeans first arrived.

How was a tepee made?

A TEPEE WAS HOME FOR THE NATIVE AMERICANS OF THE GREAT Plains. It was made from a conical framework of poles covered with buffalo hides. It was ideal for the nomadic life style of the Plains peoples because it was easy to take down, easy to transport, and easy to put up again.

Where did the West begin?

As the settlers saw it, the Western frontier moved slowly westwards with them into North America. In the 1600s, the "West" was anywhere beyond the Appalachian Mountains—unknown and dangerous. By the early 1800s, European settlement had pushed westwards as far as the Mississippi, but beyond that was a wild and unfamiliar country. The expeditions of explorers such as Meriwether Lewis and William Clark, and John C. Frémont gradually opened up this wild land, and by the 1840s, pioneer families were beginning to make the long trek westwards to a new land and a new life.

Who and what lived on the Great Plains?

The Great Plains extend from the Mississippi River westwards to the Rocky Mountains. The plains were covered with endless acres of prairie grass which was home to many animals, but particularly buffalo. Tribes such as the Pawnee and Crow lived on the Great Plains, following the herds of buffalo on which they depended for their livelihoods.

These fabulous gold objects were made by the Inca people of Peru.

What strange sight did the Zunis see?

ONE DAY IN THE SUMMER OF 1540, THE ZUNI TRIBE LOOKED OUT FROM their clifftop town and saw a procession of people approaching across the desert. Most of the people were Native Americans, but there were also many paler-faced men wearing shiny metal breastplates and riding creatures never before seen by the Zunis—horses. At the head of this caravan was the Spanish conquistador (conqueror) Francisco Vásquez de Coronado.

What were the Spaniards looking for?

Gold! Coronado and the other conquistadors were searching for the "Seven Cities of Gold," great cities dripping in gold, silver, and precious jewels. Tales of such places had been brought back by conquistadors such as Alvar Núñez Cabeza de Vaca, the first European to reach the American West when he was shipwrecked there in 1528. There was also the evidence of the great riches seized from the Aztec Empire in Mexico by Hernando Cortés after 1519, and the almost unbelievable wealth plundered from the Incas in South America by Francisco Pizarro after 1532.

Did Coronado find gold?

No. Despite spending two years looking for the fabled "Seven Cities of Gold," Coronado and his expedition found only desert, endless plains, and small scruffy villages. He returned to Mexico "very sad and very weary, completely worn out...."

Coronado and his men search for the "Seven Cities of Gold."

Which animal changed the lives of the Native Americans?

Before the arrival of Europeans, Native Americans had never before seen a horse. The arrival of the horse transformed life for many Native American people. Apache and Navajo warriors were among the first to acquire horses, but herds of horses spread rapidly across the West and horses were traded from one tribe to another. Soon, horses were used for transport, for hunting buffalo, and for war.

Who went with Coronado?

The great army of people following Coronado that day in 1540 included about 300 Spanish adventurers—at least three of whom were women. There were over 1,000 Native Americans in the service of Coronado, as well as several Franciscan priests. There were also about 1,500 horses and other pack animals carrying supplies for the huge expedition.

What happened to the Zunis?

Coronado ordered the Zunis to surrender peacefully to him, but their reply was to shoot arrows and hurl stones. However, they were no match for the Spanish horses, lances, and guns, and the Zunis were quickly overpowered. The expedition took over the Zunis' settlement and stole their food—but to their disappointment the conquistadors found no gold or treasure.

What was the silent killer the Europeans brought with them?

Guns and horses may have terrified the Native Americans who first came in contact with Europeans, but the invaders carried with them a far more dangerous threat—disease. The Native Americans had no resistance to European diseases such as smallpox, cholera, measles, and tuberculosis, and sickness spread rapidly through many tribes killing millions of Native Americans.

Where was El Pueblo de Nuestra Señora la Reina de los Angeles?

Today the city with this very long name, which means "the village of our lady the queen of the angels," is better known as Los Angeles. It was founded by a group of pioneers in 1781, built in a virtual desert, but the settlers used water from the foothills of the Sierra Nevada mountains to grow crops and raise livestock.

Who was Francisco Vásquez de Coronado?

Francisco Vásquez de Coronado (1510–1554) was one of the Spanish soldiers who went to the "New World" to seek their fortunes in the 1500s.

Which Europeans first saw the Grand Canyon?

Some members of Coronado's party traveled northwest from the Zuni settlements to search for treasure. Instead of precious metals and jewels they came across a gorge vast beyond their wildest dreams. They were the first Europeans to see the Grand Canyon.

Meriwether Lewis (left) and William Clark.

Who were Lewis and Clark?

Meriwether Lewis was the man chosen by Thomas Jefferson, third President of the United States, to lead an important expedition. Once he had been appointed, Lewis asked his friend William Clark to join him as co-leader. Together they headed a group of soldiers, explorers, and others who made up the Corps of Discovery. The task of the expedition was to travel through the territory that lay west of the Mississippi River finding out about the land, the people, the rivers—anything of interest about this vast, unknown country.

How did the Corps travel?

The Corps of Discovery set off on their journey up the Missouri River. They traveled in a large boat, called a keelboat. It was 55 ft (17 m) long, and could float in very shallow water. There were a few cabins, but most of the crew lived and slept on the open deck, covered by canvas. The keelboat could be sailed if the wind was in the right direction, rowed or towed along by human power if not. The expedition also had two large canoes, pirogues, which were each about 50 ft (15 m) long.

Why did Lewis and Clark make the incredible journey?

President Jefferson was delighted about the purchase of Louisiana, but the only problem was that he did not really know what he had bought. No one knew the exact size of Louisiana, and the only information about the land came from fur trappers. This is why Jefferson decided to send Lewis and Clark on their historic journey.

Who needed a collapsible boat?

Lewis took a collapsible boat for use later on in the expedition. He knew that the keelboat and pirogues would be left behind at some point, so he carefully designed an iron framework, which was packed into crates. Unfortunately, when the boat was eventually put together it would not float, and Lewis was forced to abandon it.

How many people were there in the Corps?

When it set off, the Corps probably numbered around 40 to 50 people, but we do not know for certain exactly how many. It included soldiers, several boatmen, a hunter named George Drouillard, and Clark's slave named York, as well as Lewis's large Newfoundland dog.

What did they take to eat?

Not much. Lewis and Clark took some provisions with them, but they were meant for emergencies only. They planned to hunt and fish for their food, and to barter with the Native Americans they met on the way.

Where did they set off from?

The Corps spent the winter in a camp just outside St Louis, where the Missouri and the Mississippi rivers meet. They set off on their famous journey on the afternoon of May 14, 1804.

Who bought Louisiana?

In one of the biggest bargains in history—the Louisiana Purchase— Jefferson bought a vast area of land west of the Mississippi River and north of the Gulf of Mexico. This region was called Louisiana, and Jefferson paid the French $15 million for it. This purchase in 1803 more than doubled the size of the United States.

Who took a medal of peace?

One of the aims of the expedition was to find out about the Native Americans living in the newly purchased Louisiana Territory. Lewis and Clark had strict instructions from President Jefferson to keep up good relations with the Native Americans they met on the journey. The expedition took many goods to offer as gifts to the Native Americans including beads, mirrors, combs, ribbons, cloth, knives, and fishhooks. There was also a special peace medal which showed hands clasped in friendship on one side, and President Jefferson on the other.

Lewis and Clark took presents to give to the Native Americans they met on their expedition.

What helped the expedition?

In August 1805, the expedition entered territory under the control of the Shoshone tribe. At first the Shoshone were very suspicious of the explorers. But just when things began to look rather threatening, Sacajawea suddenly recognized the Shoshone chief – it was her brother whom she had not seen since her kidnapping! There was great rejoicing as the two were reunited.

How did the expedition celebrate Christmas?

Christmas 1805 was spent in the confined quarters of Fort Clatsop. The explorers gave each other small gifts such as wool clothing, a Native American basket, a silk handkerchief, and moccasins. They celebrated with singing and dancing, and a week later greeted the New Year with a salute fired from their rifles into the air.

How long were Lewis and Clark away?

The Corps of Discovery were away for nearly two and a half years and they traveled over 4,300 m (7,000 km). They sailed up the Missouri River, crossed the fearsome Rocky Mountains, and braved the rapids of the mighty Columbia River before reaching the Pacific Ocean in what is present-day Oregon. They spent the winter of 1805–1806 in Fort Clatsop on the Pacific coast. The outward journey took 18 months but the journey home took only six months! The Corps of Discovery arrived back in St Louis on September 23, 1806 to the cheers of the townspeople.

Who was Sacajawea?

The first winter of the expedition (1804–1805), the Corps built a fort near the villages of the Mandan tribe. During their stay at Fort Mandan, Lewis and Clark hired a French-Canadian trader called Toussaint Charbonneau and his wife Sacajawea. Their baby son, Jean Baptiste, also joined the expedition. Sacajawea was a Native American of the Shoshone tribe who had been kidnapped as a child. As a result of her local knowledge and contacts she quickly became a vital member of the Corps of Discovery.

Sacajawea, the expedition's Native American guide, points the way.

What does Nez Perce mean?

Nez Perce was the name given by French traders to a native American tribe that lived in the Rocky Mountains. It means "pierced nose"—the members of this tribe wore ornaments through their noses. Nez Perce guides gave vital help to the Corps as they traveled through the mountains.

What happened at the Short and Long Narrows?

IN OCTOBER 1805, THE EXPEDITION REACHED THE MIGHTY COLUMBIA River. By this time the Corps was traveling in five dugout canoes. When the water became too rough for the canoes, the explorers had to pull them out and carry them and all their equipment to a calmer part of the river. But when they reached the Short and Long Narrows—a terrifying stretch of rapids between towering cliffs—there was little choice but to continue through the boiling waters. Despite their unwieldy canoes, the brave explorers survived—to the astonishment of the local Native Americans!

Who shot Meriwether Lewis?

One day, while out hunting, a short-sighted member of the expedition saw a movement in the grass and shot at what he thought was an elk. Unfortunately it turned out to be his commanding officer, Meriwether Lewis! Luckily the wound was not dangerous, and it healed rapidly over the next few weeks.

What animals did the expedition meet?

The members of the Corps of Discovery came across a bewildering array of wildlife during the expedition. They saw vast herds of antelope, buffalo, and elk, and described some frightening encounters with grizzly bears. They investigated the burrows of prairie dogs, watched Bighorn sheep walk across seemingly vertical cliff faces, and shot a Californian condor with a wingspan of nearly 10 ft (3 m).

Was the expedition a success?

The short answer is yes! The expedition returned safely, with the loss of only one member. Lewis and Clark made maps of the territory they crossed, and described hundreds of plants and animals previously unknown to Americans. And, as instructed by President Jefferson, the Corps struck up peaceful relations with the Native Americans they met on their journey.

Who were the mountain men?

THE MOUNTAIN MEN WERE FUR TRAPPERS. THEY CAUGHT ANIMALS SUCH AS beavers and sea otters for their pelts. These fur trappers were hard men. They frequently spent weeks alone in the mountains, traveling on foot and by canoe, camping in makeshift shelters, scavenging for food, and with only a rifle for protection against attacks from grizzly bears. Mountain men came from all backgrounds and from all over the globe: there were French, Russian, English, and American trappers as well as many Native Americans and some African Americans.

What did a mountain man wear?

Not surprisingly, many mountain men wore furs themselves. They often dressed in homemade clothes of fur and buckskin which were warm, comfortable, and easy to repair. Such clothes also provided excellent camouflage in the wild.

How did the mountain men survive the winters?

The main times for trapping were spring and autumn. The summer was the time for the annual rendezvous. Winter was spent lying low in camp, trading, mending traps, and waiting for the spring—the best time for trapping because the beavers still had their thick, luxurious winter coats.

A fur trapper heads up into the mountains. His horses are loaded with supplies to help him survive for weeks or even months.

What was a rendezvous?

Every summer, the mountain men would take their season's haul of pelts to a gathering known as a rendezvous. This was a kind of trade fair where the trappers would sell or barter their precious furs for money, supplies for the coming year and other goods. Once the serious bargaining was over, these gatherings often turned into wild parties. After the rendezvous, many trappers would return to the mountains having spent much of their year's income on drink, tobacco, and gambling!

Where did the furs go?

The beaver pelts were sent to the east coast of America and to Europe. Beaver fur was highly prized for making soft, waterproof felt, which was then used to make all sorts of hats. It was also used to trim ladies' coats and dresses. It was the height of fashion until the late 1830s, when styles in the big cities began to change and silk became all the rage. As demand fell, more and more of the mountain men found themselves out of work.

A trapper setting his beaver traps.

Who was Kit Carson?

KIT CARSON (1809–1868) WAS A FAMOUS MOUNTAIN MAN WHO WORKED IN the fur trade for over 10 years. In 1842 he was hired as a guide to the expeditions led by John C. Frémont, which explored much of Oregon and California.

What happened to the mountain men?

After the collapse of the fur trade, many mountain men were out of a job. Some returned to normal life in the east; others made use of their knowledge of the geography and ways of the West and became guides for explorers such as John C. Frémont, or for wagon trains of pioneer families.

How did Lewis and Clark help the fur trade?

After the success of the expedition of the Corps of Discovery, a New York merchant called John Jacob Astor decided to set up fur trading posts all along the route of the expedition. Astor created the American Fur Company in 1808, and the Pacific Fur Company in 1810. He founded a settlement called Astoria at the mouth of the Columbia River, near where Lewis and Clark had spent the winter in Fort Clatsop.

What replaced beaver?

Beaver fur may have gone out of fashion in the 1830s and 1840s, but there was still a demand for buffalo hide to make buffalo robes. Many Native Americans on the Great Plains, west of the Missouri River, hunted buffalo and sold their hides to organizations such as the American Fur Company.

A Mormon pioneer family outside their cabin in Echo City, Utah, in 1869.

On June 27, 1844, in the town of Nauvoo, Illinois, an angry mob broke into the local jail, dragged out a man named Joseph Smith and shot him dead. Smith was the founder and leader of the Church of Jesus Christ of Latter Day Saints —the Mormons. Smith and his followers had been persecuted ever since the founding of the Mormon Church in 1830, and they had already been forced to move from New York State to Ohio, to Missouri, and then to Illinois when Smith was murdered.

Who followed Brigham Young?

AFTER SMITH'S DEATH, HIS PLACE AS LEADER OF THE MORMONS WAS taken by Brigham Young. He knew that Smith had plans to move his people once more, to the wide open spaces of the Great Basin beneath the Rocky Mountains. He decided to put this plan into action, and when the Mormons were hounded out of Nauvoo in 1846, he led about 12,000 people along the Mormon Trail, across the Mississippi River, through Iowa and Nebraska, and across the Rockies.

Why was Joseph Smith murdered?
One of the beliefs of the Mormon religion was that a man could marry more than one wife. This is known as polygamy. This practice upset people wherever the Mormons went, and led to Smith's brutal murder in Nauvoo, Illinois.

Who said "This is the place"?
In August 1847, a small party of Mormons led by Brigham Young stopped on an arid, treeless plateau. Looking around him, Young said: "This is the place." This was the Great Salt Lake valley, and it was here that the Mormons founded Salt Lake City, in present-day Utah.

How did the Mormons survive?
When the Mormons arrived in the inhospitable land chosen to be their home, they had to work extremely hard to survive. Under Young's leadership they dug irrigation channels, using water from the surrounding hills to water their crops. Fifty years later, much of the barren desert had been transformed into a fruitful land.

Who was killed in the Mountain Meadows Massacre?

Where was Deseret?

The Kingdom of Deseret, meaning "Land of the Honey Bee" was the name that the Mormons gave to their new homeland. Young wanted to extend Deseret westwards to the Pacific Ocean, but the U.S. government had other ideas. Instead, the state of Utah was created in 1850, with reduced boundaries.

In 1857 THE MORMONS WERE ON THE LOOKOUT FOR GOVERNMENT troops. In September, a wagon train passed through Mormon territory and, convinced that it was a threat, the Mormons, helped by some Paiuté Native Americans, attacked. In fact, the wagon train was full of pioneers and over 100 of the migrants were killed.

Mormons on their long journey to Utah. They were led by Brigham Young.

What was the Utah War?

In 1852, the leaders of the Mormon Church admitted publicly for the first time that its members practised polygamy. Trouble between Mormons and nonMormons broke out, and in 1857 troops were sent to Utah. In fact, there was very little fighting in the Utah War, and it ended in 1858.

Cooking over a camp fire.

What was a "prairie schooner"?

OVER 1,000 PEOPLE SET OFF ALONG THE OREGON TRAIL IN 1843, THE start of the "Great Migration" to the West. They traveled in heavy wooden wagons called Conestoga wagons, pulled by horses, mules, or oxen. Later pioneers along the trail used lighter wagons which were known as "prairie schooners," because their white canvas tops looked rather like the sails on a ship called a schooner. The settlers packed their belongings into the wagons, as well as supplies for the journey. Only babies and sick people actually rode in the wagons—everyone else walked.

Where did the Oregon and California trails go?

In 1840, there were fewer than 150 Americans living in the vast area in the American West known as Oregon. Only five years later, there were thousands of American settlers in the region. Most had traveled across the continent of America along the 2,000-mile (3,200-km) Oregon Trail. This trail usually started in Independence, Missouri, crossed the Great Plains and the Rocky Mountains, and ended in the Columbia River region of Oregon. An alternative trail, the California Trail, followed the same route until Fort Hall, west of the Rocky Mountains, when it branched southwards, ending in the Sacramento valley.

Who wore bloomers?

Many pioneer women found that the heavy, full-length dresses that were the usual dress of the period were hopelessly impractical for life on the trail. Some women started to wear shorter dresses that did not reach all the way to the ground; others even dared to wear "bloomers"—a type of pants.

How many wagons were there in a wagon train?

Settlers traveled in groups along the trail for safety and for companionship, and there could be anything up to 100 wagons in a wagon train. The train traveled very slowly—at little over 1 mph (1.5 kph) and was on the move for nine or 10 hours every day.

A pioneer wagon loaded with a family's possessions.

Who was in charge of the train?

In the spring, groups of pioneers met in rendezvous towns such as Independence or St Joseph, Missouri or Council Bluffs, Iowa. They formed wagon-train companies and elected a leader, known as the raid captain. They also employed guides to lead them along the trail.

What happened at night?

At the end of a long day on the trail, the wagons would draw up into circles and set up camp for the night. These wagon circles gave the settlers protection in case of attack from Native Americans.

What did the men do?

The men in a wagon train were in charge of driving and repairing their wagons and looking after their livestock. They also hunted for food, and took turns standing guard at night, keeping watch for hostile Native Americans.

What were the women's jobs?

During the long, arduous journey, the women on a wagon train were in charge of preparing food —rising before dawn to ensure that a fire was lit and food was ready. They also washed and mended clothes, and looked after the children and sick people.

The Oregon Trail and the California Trail both began in Independence, Missouri.

How long was the journey?

The journey from Missouri to Oregon took about eight months, usually starting in April. It was vital to get through the coastal mountain ranges (the Cascades and the Sierra Nevada) before the winter snows set in. But starting out too early was dangerous too—settlers ran the risk that there would not be enough grass for their livestock to eat.

Why did so many pioneers die?

THOUSANDS OF PEOPLE DIED ALONG THE OREGON AND CALIFORNIA TRAILS.

One estimate is that seven people died for every mile of the route. The biggest killer was disease, particularly cholera. However, the greatest fear for the pioneers was attack from Native Americans. In fact, very few people died as a result of such attacks.

John Sutter. The California Gold Rush began when gold was found by one of his workers.

Was it real gold?

When Marshall found the yellow rocks in the millstream he immediately rushed to find his employer, John Sutter. There was just one question on the mens' minds: Was this real gold? After trying out various tests on the precious nuggets there was no doubt. In fact, Sutter was not happy with Marshall's discovery. He did not actually own the land on which the sawmill was built, and feared that his estate would be overrun by gold-seekers—which is exactly what happened.

How do we know Marshall did find the gold?

An entry in the diary of one of the workmen working at Sutter's Mill agrees with Marshall's story of the discovery of the gold. It reads: "This day some kind of mettle [metal] was found in the tail race that looks like goald [gold]. First discovered by James Martial [Marshall], the Boss of the Mill."

How did the secret get out?

Marshall and Sutter tried to keep their discovery a secret. But, while Sutter tried unsuccessfully to claim the land on which the sawmill stood, rumor started to spread. At first, workers at the sawmill did some quiet prospecting, then their neighbors joined in, then the news began to spread further.

What did President Polk show to Congress?

At first, not everyone believed in the wild tales of gold coming from the West. Many people back East dismissed the tales as fanciful rumors. But in December 1848, President Polk showed a tea box full of gold dust to Congress— proof that the rumors were true!

Who found gold in California?

ON A JANUARY MORNING IN 1848, A CARPENTER CALLED JAMES

Marshall was sent by his employer, John Sutter, to inspect some work on a sawmill. The mill was on a bend of the America River in California. As Marshall inspected a ditch dug out of the bed of the millstream, he noticed something glittering on the bottom. He bent down and saw several golden-yellow rocks, about the size of small peas. Marshall had found gold!

Who was Sam Brannan?

STOREKEEPER SAM BRANNAN WAS DETERMINED THAT EVERYONE SHOULD know about the goldfields. In May 1848, he galloped through the streets of San Francisco waving his hat and shouting: "Gold! Gold from the America River!" Within a few weeks, three out of four men in the town had gone to look for gold.

Where did the prospectors come from?

Once the news of gold reached San Francisco it traveled like wildfire—across California, north to Oregon, south as far as Peru and Chile, and across the Pacific Ocean to Hawaii. In the spring and summer of 1848, gold-seekers began to pour into the area— and it seemed that there was plenty of gold for everyone.

Which gold-finders died very poor?

Marshall and Sutter both died in poverty. Marshall spent the rest of his life wandering through the hills of California looking for more gold, but with little success. Sutter saw his estate overrun with gold-seekers, as he had predicted. After several unsuccessful prospecting ventures he moved to Pennsylvania and died, heartbroken, in 1880.

How did Sam Brannan make his fortune?

Why was Sam Brannan so eager to spread the news about the gold? He was a clever tradesman who owned several stores selling hardware, such as picks and shovels. Brannan realized that there was a fortune to be made selling his supplies to the thousands of gold-seekers—and he did become a very rich man.

A prospector panning for gold in a stream in California.

Who were the "forty-niners"?

ONCE PRESIDENT POLK HAD PROVED THAT THERE REALLY WAS A goldmine in the American West, the "Gold Rush" began. In 1849, about 90,000 people headed for California from all over the globe. They became known as the "forty-niners."

An early advert for Levi jeans.

How did the gold seekers get to California?

There were many different routes to reach the goldfields—all dangerous. Many people walked overland—some as far as 2,000 miles (3,300 km). Others went by sea to Panama, traveled overland to the Pacific Ocean and continued to San Francisco by sea. Many died before they reached California.

A poster advertising voyages from New York to San Francisco in California. Sailing was the quickest way to get there – and the most expensive.

Who wrote: "Go West, young man, go West!"?

These words appeared in an American newspaper editorial in 1851. By that time, many thousands of hopeful gold-seekers had already headed West across the American continent in the hope of making their fortunes. Most of them were men who left behind their homes and families, intending to return after a few months or years, rich beyond their wildest dreams. Very few succeeded.

What did a shout of: "Color!" mean?

It meant that the prospectors had struck lucky and found gold. The early prospectors discovered gold quite easily on the beds of rivers and streams. They used a flat "pan" to swirl a mixture of gravel and water around until the lighter gravel was washed away, leaving the heavier gold behind. But as time went on, finding gold became harder. Prospectors had to dig deeper using long wooden boxes called cradles to sort the mud and gravel from any gold.

Where did barmen find gold?

The answer is on the floor of the bar! Many miners used pinches of gold dust to pay for refreshment, and after a long night of serving drinks, barmen in California would pan the floor of the saloon to pick up any gold that had fallen there!

What did Levi Strauss sell to the prospectors?

Levi Strauss was a German immigrant living in New York when the Gold Rush started. He traveled to the West and sold cotton material which he advertised as ideal for making tents. However, it turned out to be rather more suitable for pants—the first Levis.

Where were Lousy Ravine and Bogus Thunder?

THESE ARE BOTH NAMES OF GOLD-MINING CAMPS IN CALIFORNIA, LONG since abandoned. Names of gold camps and towns often told their own stories, such as You Bet, Git-Up-and-Git, and Bedbug!

How much did an egg cost?
When they arrived in California, prospectors were amazed at the high price of food and supplies. One egg cost as much as $3. Everything—from accommodation to picks and shovels—was overpriced, and the gold-seekers had little choice but to pay up.

What are ghost towns?
Today, you can see many reminders of the Gold Rush in the American West. The gold miners built camps and towns wherever they struck gold, and they abandoned them just as quickly when the gold ran out. Many of these towns survive as "ghost towns"—empty and in ruins.

These prospectors are using a "long tom" to search for gold. The running water separated out pieces of gold from dirt, stones and other waste.

Who built the railroad across America?

I N 1862, CONGRESS PASSED AN ACT TO
AUTHORIZE THE CONSTRUCTION
of a railroad (railway) that would link the east and the west
coasts of America. Two companies were given the contracts
to build the railroad. The Union Pacific started in Omaha,
Nebraska, and worked westwards. The Central Pacific
started in Sacramento, west of the Sierra Nevada
mountains, and worked eastwards. Construction of the
tracks started in 1863 and took over five years to complete.

What happened when the companies met?
The two bands of workers came face to face in Utah, and at first they kept
building—each side refusing to stop building in the hope of getting extra
pay for the extra mile or two! The government stepped in to order the line
to meet at Promontory Summit—but not before a few fights had broken
out between the rival workers.

The railroad linked the east and west coasts of
the United States.

What happened on May 10, 1869?
In May 1869, at Promontory Summit, Utah, the tracks of the Union Pacific and the Central Pacific finally met. The Governor of California and president of the Central Pacific, Leland Stanford, lifted the hammer and brought it down to hit the last spike in the track—a golden one. He missed, but the telegraph man sent the news nevertheless: "DONE!" In Washington D.C. a great cheer greeted the news, and in San Francisco, celebrations began.

Why was it a race?
The companies were paid by the government for every mile of track they laid, between $16,000 and $48,000 per mile depending on the difficulty of the terrain. They also received land on either side of the track. Not surprisingly, construction turned into a race between the two companies to see which could lay the most track.

Who worked for the Central Pacific?

Not only did the Central Pacific company have to bring its supplies by ship around South America, it also had to drive the railroad through the Sierra Nevada mountains. To do this work, thousands of laborers were recruited in China and brought to California.

How many Chinese laborers died for the railroad?

It is estimated that over 1,000 Chinese workers died during the construction of the railroad. They struggled against appalling conditions in the Sierra Nevada mountains, blasting holes with dynamite in solid rock, working in baskets precariously slung by ropes over huge drops, and cutting down giant redwood trees.

Who won the railroad race?

The Union Pacific company laid more track than the Central Pacific —but the Union Pacific workers had an easier task. Much of the eastern part of the railroad was across the Great Plains, and they had a direct supply route from the east.

Hammering in a golden spike at the point where the Union Pacific and Central Pacific railroads met.

How was the track laid?

EVERY PART OF THE TRACK WAS LAID BY HAND. ADVANCE PARTIES LEVELED out the land ready for the heavy crossways timbers, called ties. The iron rails were laid on to the timbers and attached by spikes and bolts. Only two or three miles of track were laid per day.

What did the Native Americans think of the railroad?

The railroad cut through Native Americans' land and hunters shot thousands of buffalo to feed the hungry railroad workers. The Native Americans showed their anger by attacking the construction crews.

A pioneer farmer using a horse-drawn plow to break up the soil of the prairie.

What could you get for $10 in 1862?

In 1862, the government passed the Homestead Act. Its terms promised 160 acres of land to settlers who were prepared to move to the Great Plains and farm the land for at least five years. The settlers paid $10 to register for the scheme and it encouraged thousands of families to move to the prairies to start a new life. Many traveled west on the new railroads, some from western states of the USA, others from Europe.

What was a soddy?

THE FIRST TASK FOR ANY PIONEER WAS TO BUILD A SHELTER FOR

protection against the searingly hot summer sun and the icy winter blast on the prairies. The quickest way of making a shelter was to make a dugout in the side of a hill, using the excavated earth to make a wall at the front of the cave. In the spring, pioneers made houses from turf sods, known as soddies. The inside walls of these houses were lined with clay.

A pioneer family outside their sod house, or "soddy."

Why were windmills important?

Life on the Great Plains would have been impossible without windmills. Water was very scarce on the surface of the prairies, so it had to be drawn from underground wells. The constant winds turned the mills and pumped water from deep underground.

Who bought wheat with them?

In 1874, immigrants from the Crimea region of Russia brought with them a particularly hardy type of wheat, called Turkey Red. They planted it on their new farms in Kansas and it flourished. In a short time, the region had became the major wheat-producing region of the United States.

What hardships did the pioneers face?

Life on the prairies was very hard for the early pioneer farmers. Winters were bitterly cold and summers baking hot. Fire was a constant danger, as well as tornadoes, droughts and, in spring, floods. There were also plagues of insects such as grasshoppers, which got everywhere and ate everything.

Were children expected to work?

EVERYONE IN THE PIONEER FAMILY HAD TO WORK HARD SIMPLY TO SURVIVE, and children were no exception. They gathered buffalo dung for fuel, fed the animals, fetched water, and weeded vegetable gardens. During harvest, children helped their parents in the fields.

What kind of plow did the pioneers use?

The soil of the prairies was heavy and difficult to plow at first. The pioneers used a heavy steel plow that was invented by John Deere in 1837. This plow was strong enough to cut through the heavy soil and to turn it over.

Where did the pioneers come from?

Many pioneers came from Europe, drawn by the offer of free land and a chance to start afresh. They came from Norway and Russia, Scotland, France, the Netherlands and Ireland. Some English pioneers bought land in Kansas, but after a few years most of them had returned home.

What was barbed wire used for?

There were few trees on the prairies, so wood was very scarce. Without wood, the pioneers planted prickly hedges to fence off their farmland. But the invention of barbed wire in the early 1870s made fencing much better.

A cowboy trail boss in Montana, 1888.

What was a trail drive?

Trail drives started in the south, in Texas near the Gulf of Mexico. Two or three thousand cattle were rounded up and then driven day after day, week after week, northwards to the nearest railroad junction. The first of these railroad links was Abilene in Kansas. The trail drive from Texas to Abilene took about three months and it became known as the Chisholm Trail. The earliest trail drives were in 1867, when an estimated 35,000 cattle made the journey along the Chisholm Trail.

What was life like on a trail drive?

Trail drives lasted three or four months and, at first, the cowboys had to live on what they could carry and cook for themselves. They ate mostly beans and hard bread. Later, when trail drives became more organized, a chuck wagon accompanied the cowboys carrying food, water and other supplies.

What was a ranch?

As the cattle business boomed, some Texas cattlemen set up large farms, known as ranches. The ranch owner employed cowboys to work full-time looking after his cattle. The owner lived in a house in the center of the ranch; the cowboys often lived in bunkhouses.

Why did the cattle move so slowly?

On the trail, it was important not to drive the cattle too hard. They needed to arrive at the railhead in good condition. On the journey, the cattle grazed on the grass that was freely available across the Great Plains. As well as the Chisholm, there were several other trails including the Shawnee, the Western and the Goodnight-Loving Trail.

What was a bronco?

ONE OF A COWBOY'S JOBS ON THE RANCH WAS TO BREAK IN untamed horses, called broncos. A wild horse was caught with a lassoo. It was then up to the cowboy to blindfold and saddle the horse before getting into the saddle. The horse would then start bucking and rearing, trying to throw the cowboy from its back. Many cowboys were injured trying to tame broncos.

Who was Joseph G. McCoy?

It is claimed that McCoy was the first person to organize a trail drive. He recruited experienced cowboys from Texas to drive the herds northwards. In Texas the cattle would fetch no more than $4 a head: in Kansas the price was nearer $40!

What did cowboys wear?

HIGH-HEELED BOOTS, leather "chaps" for the legs, wide-brimmed Stetson hat, a lassoo, and a cowboy saddle were the distinctive trademarks of a cowboy. The cattle business had long been established in Mexico and the southern United States, but the arrival of the railroads saw the beginning of a new era. Now, cattle could be driven across the Great Plains to the nearest railroad link, then transported to markets in the east and the north where they fetched high prices. And with the cattle came the cowboys.

Why were cattle branded?
So that they could identify which cattle belonged to which ranch, they were branded. This involved burning a special mark into the hide of the cow with a hot metal iron. Every ranch had its own identifying mark. An unmarked cow was known as a maverick.

A cowboy in his working clothes.

How old were cowboys?
The average age of a cowboy was 24. Many cowboys were Mexicans, or African Americans, and most earned no more than $30 a month. Their lives were incredibly tough. They owned their clothes, precious saddles, and guns but little else, although a few also had their own horses.

Who was Billy the Kid?

A NOTORIOUS OUTLAW, BILLY THE KID WAS SAID TO HAVE KILLED 27 people before his early death at the age of 21. It is hard to know who he was—in his early years he went by the name of Henry McCarty; Later he called himself William H. Bonney Jr.

How did bandits hold up a train?

One classic Wild West method was to wait until night, then signal with a red lantern for the chosen train to stop. The outlaws often took over the train, driving it to a safe spot before using dynamite to open the safe where the money was stored. The explosion could blow banknotes far and wide, which the bandits would quickly collect before disappearing into the night.

Who carried out the first train robberies?

In October 1866, members of the Reno Gang held up a train on the Ohio and Mississippi Railroad, stealing more than $13,000. The Reno gang was just one of the many gangs of bandits and outlaws that terrorized the West during the pioneer years, robbing banks, stagecoaches, and trains, and stealing horses and cattle.

This Colt revolver was owned by the outlaw Jesse James.

What was the Hole-in-the-Wall?

The Hole-in-the-Wall was the name of a gorge that was home to 100 or more bandits in the 1890s. It lay about 50 m (81 km) south of Buffalo, in Wyoming. Most of the outlaws were cattle or horse thieves. They were known as the "Wild Bunch," and its most famous members were Butch Cassidy and the Sundance Kid.

Why was Belle Starr called the "Bandit Queen"?

Women, as well as men, turned to violence as a way of life in the Wild West. One of the most famous female bandits was Belle Starr. Her skill on horseback, armed with a brace of pistols, earned her the title the "Bandit Queen."

What happened in Northfield, Minnesota in 1876?

On September 7, 1876, the infamous James-Younger Gang, led by brothers Jesse and Frank James, held up the First National Bank of Northfield. But the cashier refused to open the vault where the money was kept, and the townspeople started to fire at the robbers. After a desperate battle the gang escaped—but many of its members were killed or injured.

What happened at the O.K. Corral?

IN 1881, THERE WAS A FAMOUS GUNFIGHT AT THE

O.K. Corral in Tombstone, Arizona—the result of a feud between rival gangs in the town. Involved in the fight was Wyatt Earp. He was in fact a lawman, serving as a deputy sheriff and as a U.S. marshal, but his history was as violent and colorful as that of many criminals.

The infamous Jesse James posed for this photograph in 1864. At that time, he was fighting in the American Civil War.

The Reno Gang prepare to rob a train on the move.

Was Jesse James a hero?
Many myths and romantic stories grew up about the outlaws of the Wild West. The bandit, Jesse James, was often portrayed as a Robin Hood figure who stole from the rich in order to help the poor. In fact, he was a callous and brutal thief who thought nothing of attacking and killing unarmed and defenseless people.

What were "Pinkerton men"?
Allen Pinkerton (1819–1884) set up one of the first detective agencies in the United States. His employees, known as "Pinkerton men" were responsible for capturing many outlaws, including the infamous Reno Gang.

What happened to the buffalo?

MANY NATIVE AMERICAN TRIBES THAT LIVED ON THE GREAT

Plains had long relied on the buffalo for their livelihoods. But once the railroads were built across the Plains, buffalo-hunting increased dramatically. Despite resistance from Native Americans, professional American buffalo-hunters came to the Plains in their thousands to shoot the seemingly limitless herds. In the south, over four million buffalo were shot between 1872 and 1874. In the north, the buffalo herd was destroyed in the early 1880s.

What were Native American reservations?

As more settlers moved into the American West, they often came into conflict with the native peoples who had been living on those lands for many generations. In the 1850s and 1860s, the American government made various treaties with the peoples of the Great Plains, establishing peaceful relations and promising them specific areas of land, known as reservations. Despite the treaties, there were many battles between the US army and Native American warriors who did not want to move on to the reservations.

What was buffalo hide used for?

In the 1870s there was a huge demand for buffalo hides. The hides were made into leather for shoes and other products. They were also used to make belts to drive the machinery in factories.

Who wanted the buffalo destroyed?

Some Americans thought that the destruction of the buffalo herds was a good thing because it would force rebellious Native American tribes into submission. Without the buffalo, they would be forced to rely on farming and government hand-outs for food. Other people were horrified and tried to stop the slaughter— but they failed.

Where did the Nez Perce go?

Whole tribes were forced to move thousands of miles to live on new reservations. The Nez Perce lived in the northwest, in Oregon. They tried to live peacefully with the settlers. But eventually violence erupted. The Nez Perces fought hard against the settlers, but they were eventually forced to move to a reservation far away in Oklahoma.

Millions of buffalo were killed by professional hunters in the early 1870s.

Who died at the Battle of Little Bighorn?

In June 1876, General George A. Custer led a group of soldiers to drive the defiant Sioux off their land in the Black Hills and on to a reservation. Custer found the Native Americans' camp at Little Bighorn on June 25, and decided to attack immediately. He did not know that at least 2,000 Native American warriors were in the camp, under their leaders Sitting Bull and Chief Crazy Horse. Custer and his men were defeated and killed by the Native Americans, sending shock waves through white American society.

The Sioux Reservation at Pine Ridge, South Dakota, in 1890.

Where did a gold rush cause problems?

In 1874, gold was discovered in the Black Hills of South Dakota. Unfortunately, the gold was on territory under the control of the Sioux and soon miners were flooding into the Black Hills, ignoring the Native Americans' rights over the land. Violence erupted, and the Sioux were ordered by the government to leave—but they refused.

What was the worst tragedy for the Sioux?

Over 150 Native Americans, including women and children, were massacred by the army at Wounded Knee, South Dakota. Twenty-five soldiers also died. After the massacre, the remaining Sioux had little choice but to move to the reservation set aside for them by the government.

Who danced the Ghost Dance?

IN THE DESPERATE TIMES OF THE LATE 1800S, MANY NATIVE Americans in the West turned in hope to a new movement known as the Ghost Dance. The Ghost Dance helped Native Americans to cope with the destruction of the buffalo and the loss of their lands by promising a return to the old ways of life and better times.

Index

ACKNOWLEDGEMENTS

All the photographs in this book were
supplied by Peter Newark's Pictures.